GUITAR CHORDS/LYRICS

BRANDI CARLILE
by the way, I forgive you

ISBN 978-1-5400-1565-5

HAL•LEONARD®
7777 W. BLUEMOUND RD. P.O. BOX 13819 MILWAUKEE, WI 53213

In Australia Contact:
Hal Leonard Australia Pty. Ltd.
4 Lentara Court
Cheltenham, Victoria, 3192 Australia
Email: ausadmin@halleonard.com.au

Visit Hal Leonard Online at
www.halleonard.com

when I asked the man next door Who looked as if he knew, His
don't know what the black-bird sang Or what the ro-ses said, But it
get-ting on for thir-ty-five, And still I do not know What

wife was ve-ry cross in-deed And said it would-n't do.
was-n't in the chick-en run Or un-der-neath the bed.
kind of crea-ture it can be That bo-thers peo-ple so.

($\downarrow$ = 58) (Very much $\frac{2}{2}$)

Does it look_____ like a
Can it pull_____ ex-tra-
When it comes,_____ will it

Ped.   * Ped.   * sim.

pair_____ of py - ja - mas__ Or the ham in a temp'rance ho -
-or - - din -'ry fa - ces,__ Is it u - sual - ly sick on a
come_____ with - out warn - ing _____ Just as I'm pick - ing my

-tel,_____
swing,_____
nose,_____

O tell me the truth a - bout love.

Does its o - - dour re - mind_____ one of
Does it spend_____ all its time_____ at the
Will it knock_____ on my door_____ in the

Every Time I Hear That Song

Words and Music by Brandi Carlile, Phil Hanseroth and Tim Hanseroth

Capo VII

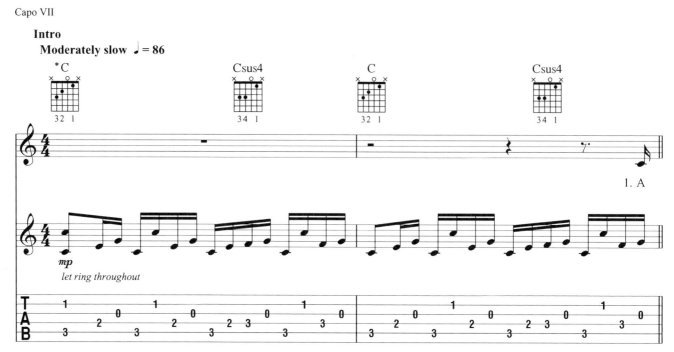

*All music sounds 3 1/2 steps higher than indicated due to capo.

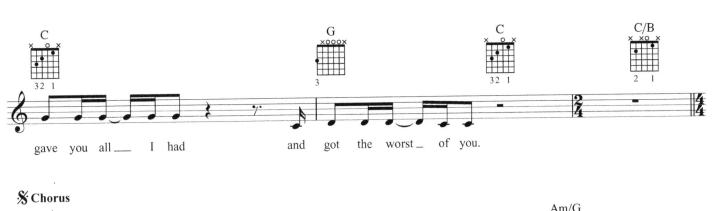

gave you all ___ I had and got the worst ___ of you.

𝄋 Chorus

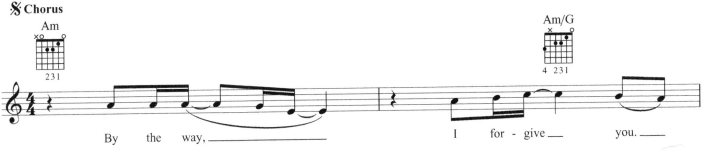

By the way, _____ I for - give ___ you. ___

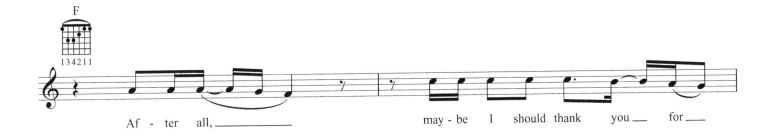

Af - ter all, _____ may - be I should thank you ___ for ___

giv - ing me what I've found, ___ be - cause with - out you a - round ___ I've been ___

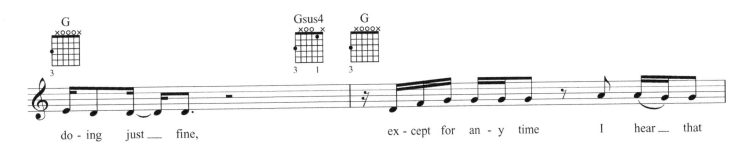

do - ing just ___ fine, ex - cept for an - y time I hear ___ that

To Coda ⊕

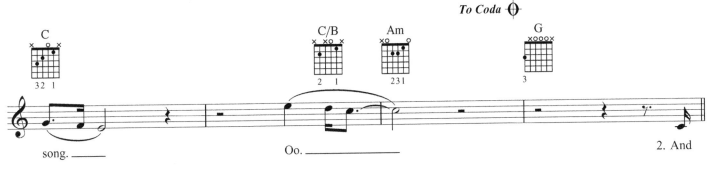

song. ___ Oo. _____ 2. And

Chorus

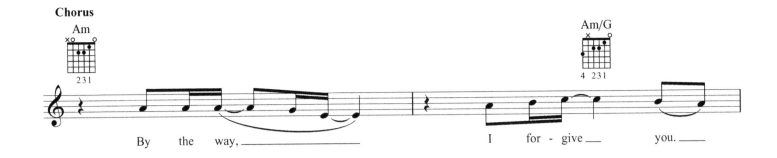

By the way, _____ I for - give ___ you. ___

Af - ter all, _____ may - be I should thank you ___ for ___

giv - ing me what I found, ___ be - cause with - out you a - round ___ I've been ___

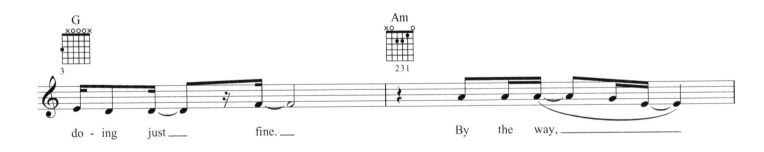

do - ing just ___ fine. ___ By the way, _____

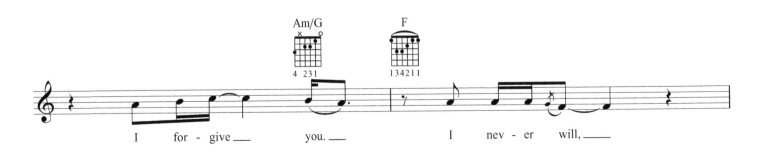

I for - give ___ you. ___ I nev - er will, ___

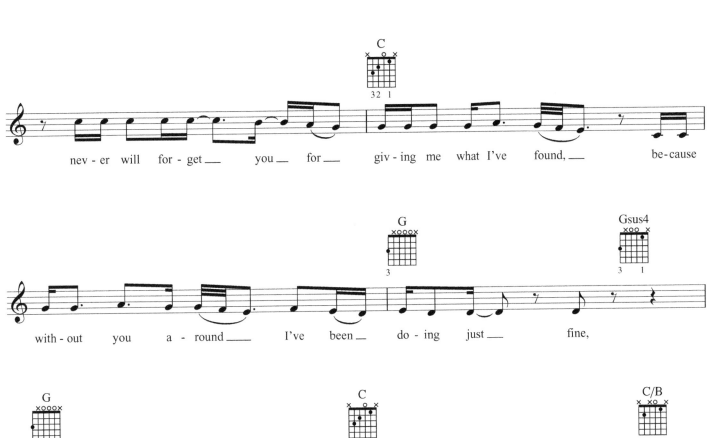

nev-er will for-get ___ you ___ for ___ giv-ing me what I've found, ___ be-cause

with-out you a-round ___ I've been ___ do-ing just ___ fine,

ex-cept for an-y time I hear ___ that song. ___ Oo. ___

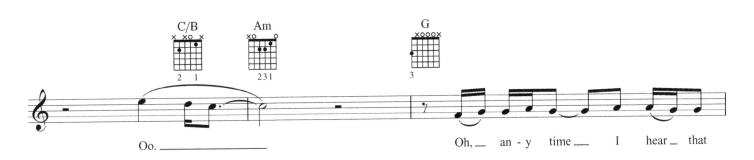

___ Oh, ___ an-y time ___ I hear ___ that song. ___

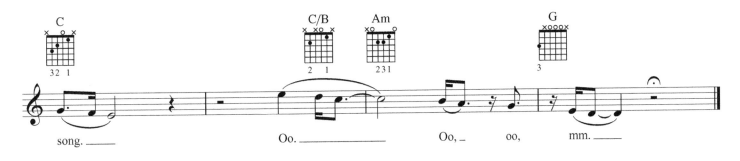

Oo. ___ Oh, ___ an-y time ___ I hear ___ that

song. ___ Oo. ___ Oo, ___ oo, ___ mm. ___

The Joke

Words and Music by Brandi Carlile, Phil Hanseroth, Tim Hanseroth and Dave Cobb

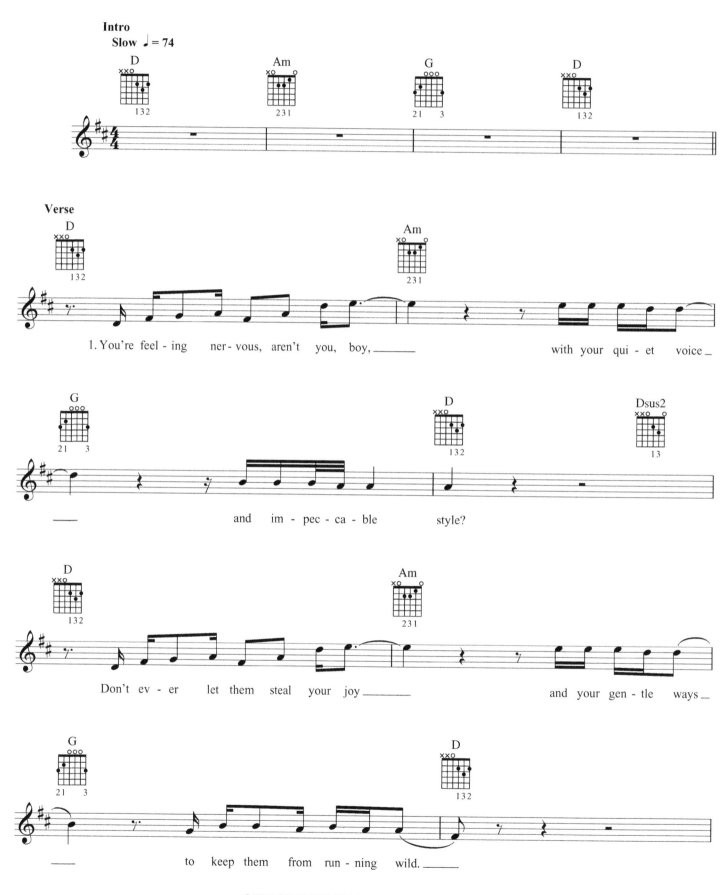

They can kick _ dirt in your face, _ dress you down _ and tell _ you that your place is in the

mid - dle when they hate the way you shine. _____

I see you tug - ging on your shirt, _____ try - ing to hide in - side _

_____ of it, and hide how _ much it hurts. _____ Let them

Chorus

laugh while _____ they can. _____ Let them

spin, let them scat - ter in _____ the wind. _

11

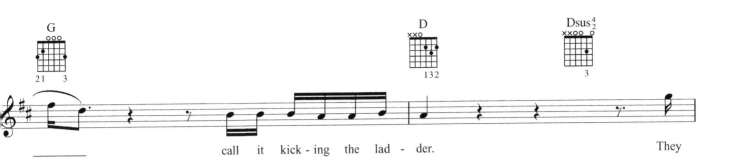

call it kick-ing the lad-der. They

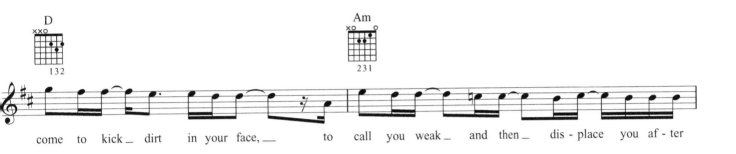

come to kick _ dirt in your face, _ to call you weak _ and then _ dis-place you af-ter

car-ry-ing your ba-by on your back a-cross _ the des-ert. _

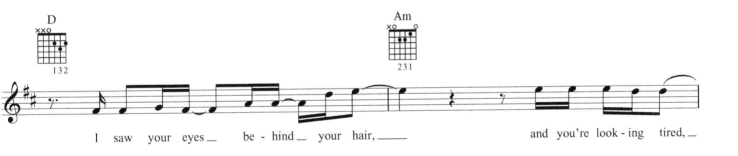

I saw your eyes _ be-hind _ your hair, _ and you're look-ing tired, _

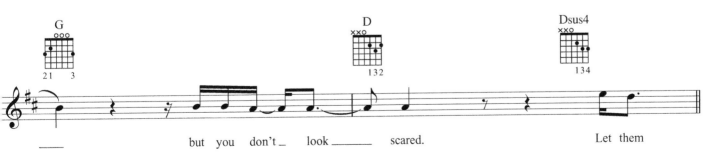

___ but you don't _ look ___ scared. Let them

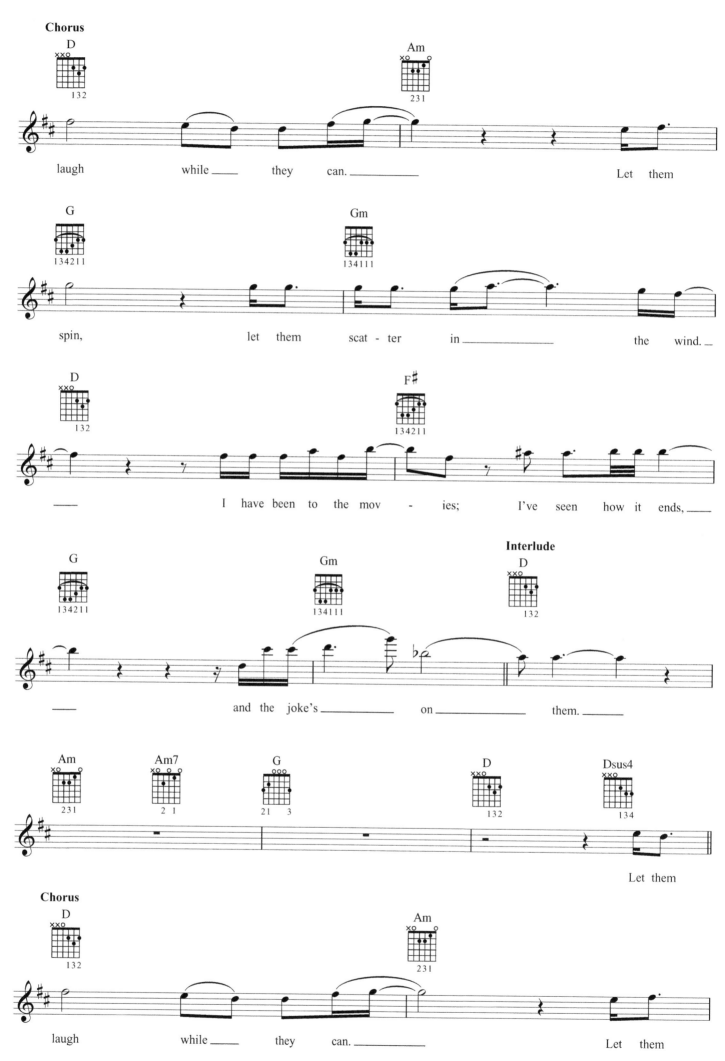

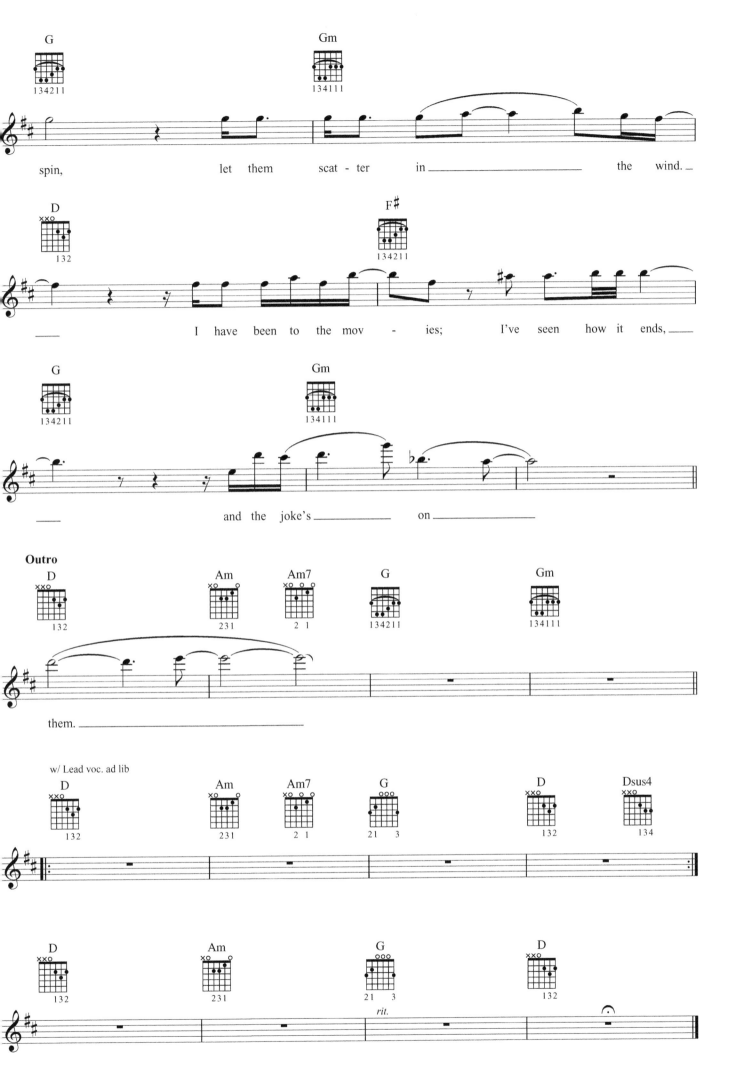

spin,   let them scat - ter   in _____ the wind. _

____   I have been to the mov - ies;   I've seen how it ends, ____

____   and the joke's _____ on _____

Outro

them. _____

w/ Lead voc. ad lib

rit.

Hold Out Your Hand

Words and Music by Brandi Carlile, Phil Hanseroth and Tim Hanseroth

%. Chorus

Half time ♩ = 128

Hold out __ your __ hand, __ take hold of mine __ and then __

__ round and round __ we go. __

Don't you want __ to dance? __ I'm a dy - ing man __

__ from the mo - ment we __ be - gan. __ Hold out __ your __

Interlude

hand.

(Ba da da, ba da da, ba da da. Ba da da, ba da da, ba da da.

To Coda

Ba da da, ba da da, ba da da.) __

2. When the

18

blaz - ing sun. ___ And the dev - il don't break for the fi - er - y snake, _____ and you've

had a - bout as god - damned much as you ___ could take. _____ The

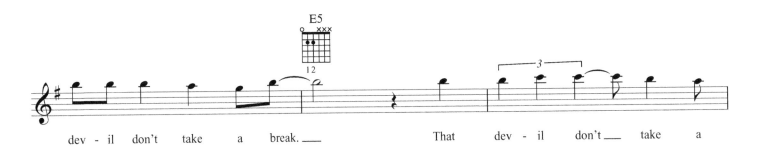

dev - il don't take a break. ___ That dev - il don't ___ take a

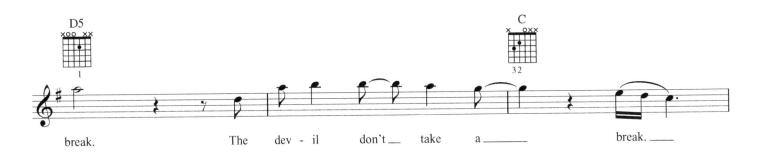

break. The dev - il don't ___ take a _____ break. ___

D.S. al Coda

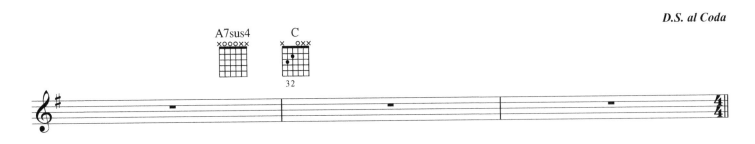

Coda

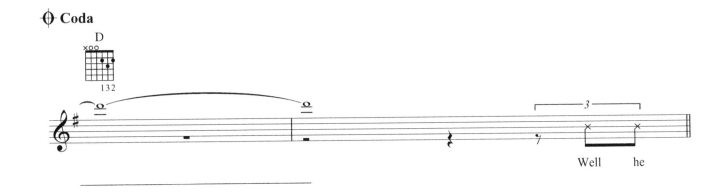

Well he

_____

Bridge

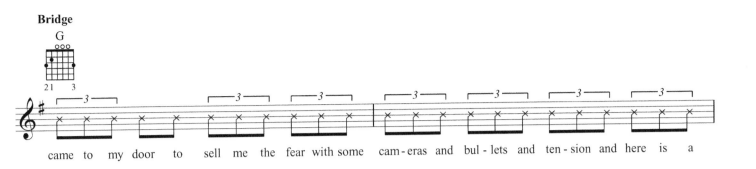

came to my door to sell me the fear with some cam-eras and bul-lets and ten-sion and here is a

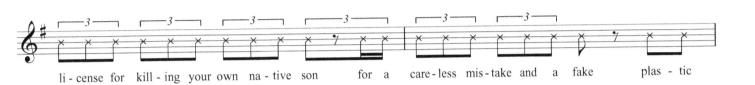

li-cense for kill-ing your own na-tive son for a care-less mis-take and a fake plas-tic

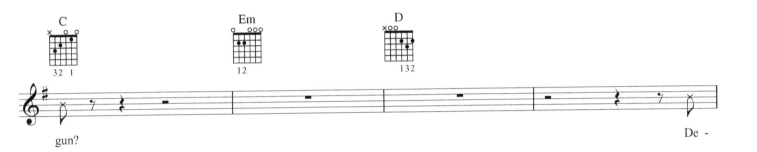

gun?   De -

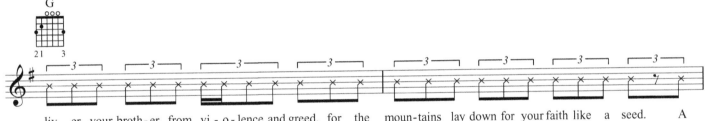

liv-er your broth-er from vi-o-lence and greed, for the moun-tains lay down for your faith like a seed.   A

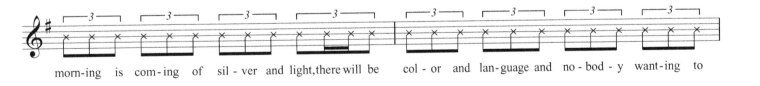

morn-ing is com-ing of sil-ver and light, there will be col-or and lan-guage and no-bod-y want-ing to

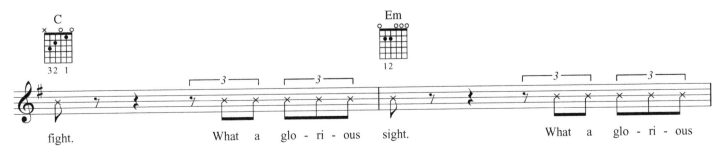

fight.   What a glo-ri-ous sight.   What a glo-ri-ous

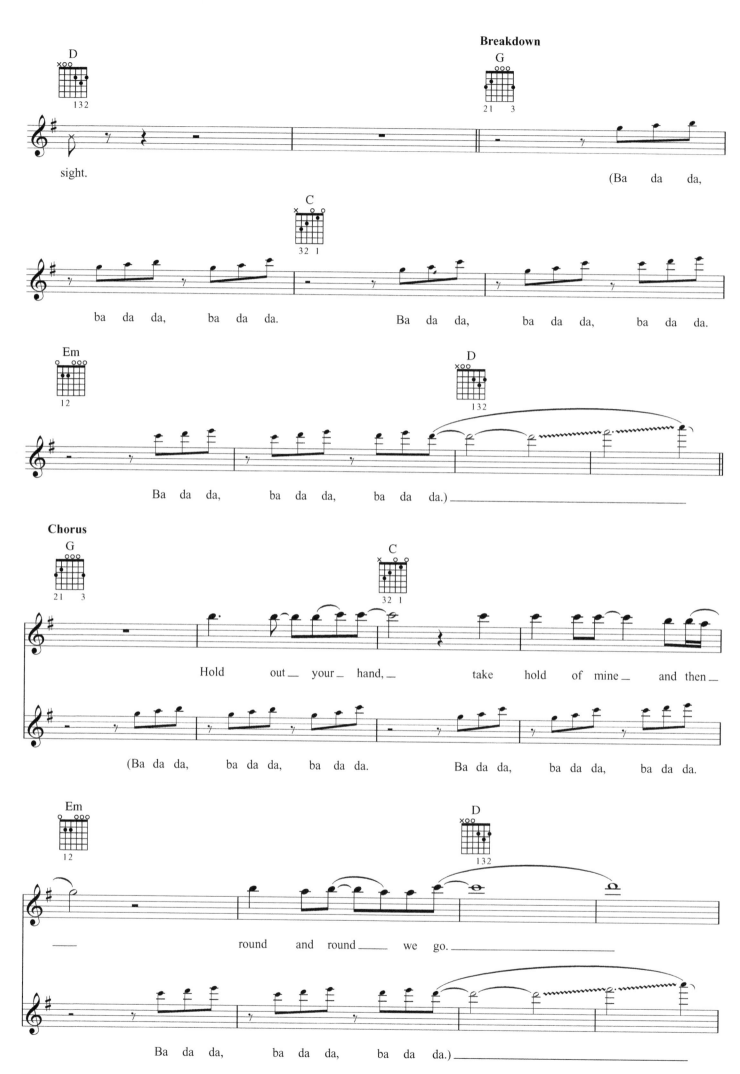

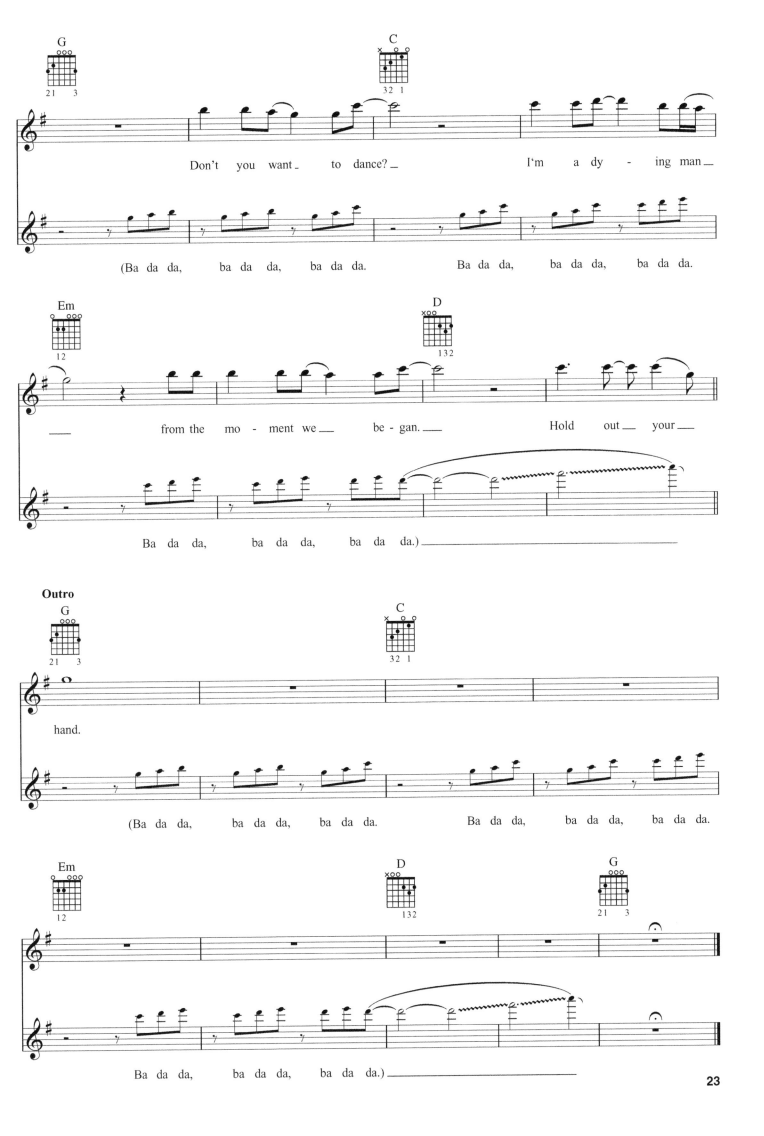

Don't you want to dance? I'm a dy - ing man

(Ba da da, ba da da, ba da da. Ba da da, ba da da, ba da da.

from the mo - ment we be - gan. Hold out your

Ba da da, ba da da, ba da da.)

Outro

hand.

(Ba da da, ba da da, ba da da. Ba da da, ba da da, ba da da.

Ba da da, ba da da, ba da da.)

The Mother

Words and Music by Brandi Carlile, Phil Hanseroth and Tim Hanseroth

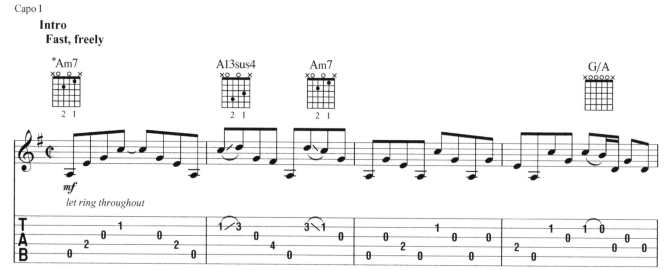

*All music sounds 1/2 step higher than indicated due to capo.

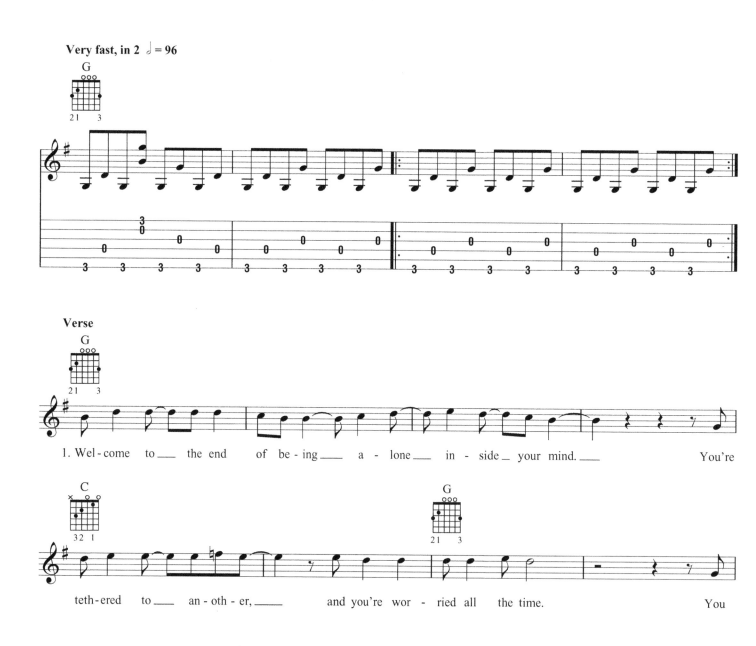

1. Wel-come to ___ the end of be-ing ___ a - lone ___ in - side ___ your mind. ___ You're
teth-ered to ___ an - oth - er, ___ and you're wor - ried all the time. You

al - ways knew__ the mel - o - dy, but__ you__ nev - er heard it___ rhyme.

2. She's

Verse

fair and she__ is qui - et,___ lord. She does - n't look like__ me. She

made me love__ the morn - ing, she's__ a hol - i - day at__ sea. The

New York streets__ are as bus - y as__ they__ al - ways used to be,

but I am the moth - er of___ E - van - ge - line. __

Interlude

3. The

world that stood a-gainst us, ____ made us ____ mean to fight for you. ____ And

when we chose ____ your name, ____ we knew ____ that you'd fight the pow - er,

too.

6. You're

Verse

noth-ing short ____ of mag - i - cal ____ and beau-ti - ful to me. I'll ____

nev - er hit ____ the big time with - out ____ you.

So

they can keep their trea - sure and their ____ ties ____ to the ma - chine

cause I am the moth - er of ____ E - van - ge - line.

5

6

fluff,_____ Is it sharp or quite smooth at the ed - ges?
-nough,_____ Are its sto - ries vul-gar but fun - ny?
bluff,_____ Will it 'al - ter my life al - to-

tell me the truth a-bout love_____ O tell me the truth a-bout love._____ 2. I
3. Your

-ge - ther?_ O tell me the truth a - bout love,_____ O

tell me the truth a-bout love,_____ O tell me the truth a-bout love.

2. Funeral blues

Stop all__ the clocks, cut off the tel - e - phone,

Pre-vent the dog from bark-ing with__ a juic-y bone, Si-

8

-lence the pia - nos___ and with muffled drum

Bring out the cof - fin, let the mourn - ers come. Let

aer - o-planes cir - cle moan - ing o - ver-head

with Ped.

Scrib - bling on   the sky   the mes - sage   He Is Dead,   Tie

crepe   bands   round   the white necks   of   the pub - lic   doves,

Let   the traf - fic   police - men wear   black   cot - ton gloves.

3. Johnny

O the val-ley in the summer when

I__ and my John Be-side the deep ri-ver__ walk on and on While the

grass__ at our feet and the birds up a-bove Whis-pered so soft__ in re-

he frowned like thun - der   and went_____ a - way.

Lento: quasi recit.

Shall I ev - er for - get   at the Grand   Op - e - ra_____

When mu-sic poured out of each won-der-ful - star?_____

Di - a-monds and pearls   hung like

i - vy__ down Ov - er each gold and sil - ver__ gown;

'O John-ny I'm in hea-ven,' I whis-pered to say:__

Tempo I

But he frowned like thunder and went__ a-way.

portato

Tempo di Valse

O, O but he was as

*con Ped.*_____ *etc.*

fair as a gar-den in flower, As slen-der and tall as the great Eif-fel Tower, When the waltz throbbed out down the long pro-me-nade O his eyes and his smile went straight to my heart; 'O mar-ry me, John-ny, I'll love and o-bey': But

he frowned like thun-der and he went _____ a - way.

portato

ossia

O last night I dreamed of you, John-ny, my lo - ver; You'd the

sun ____ on one arm and the moon ___ on the o - ther, The

sea it was blue___ and the grass it was green, ev - 'ry star rat-tled a

round tam - bou-rine; Ten thou-sand miles deep in a

pit there I lay: But you___ went a - way.

ossia   rit.

4. Calypso

p dolce
For there in the mid-dle of
poco meno p
[con Ped.]
that wai - ting hall Should be standing the one that I love best of all. If he's
stacc.
not there to meet me when I get to town, I'll stand on the pavement with
stacc.
tears roll - ing down. Dri-ver, drive fas-ter, Dri-ver, drive fas - ter. For
p dolce
cresc.
p

he is the one that I love to look on, The ac-me of kind-ness and

stacc.

per-fec - tion. He pres-ses my hand and he says he loves me Which I

stacc.

find an ad-mi-ra-ble pe-cu-li-a-ri-ty. Dri-ver, drive fas-ter,

cresc.

più animato

Dri-ver, drive fas - ter Dri-ver, drive fas-ter, drive fas-ter.

The woods_____ are bright green_____ on both sides of the line; The trees_____ have their loves_____ though they're diff-'rent from mine. But the poor fat old ban-ker in the sun-par-lour car Has no-one to love him ex-cept his ci-gar.

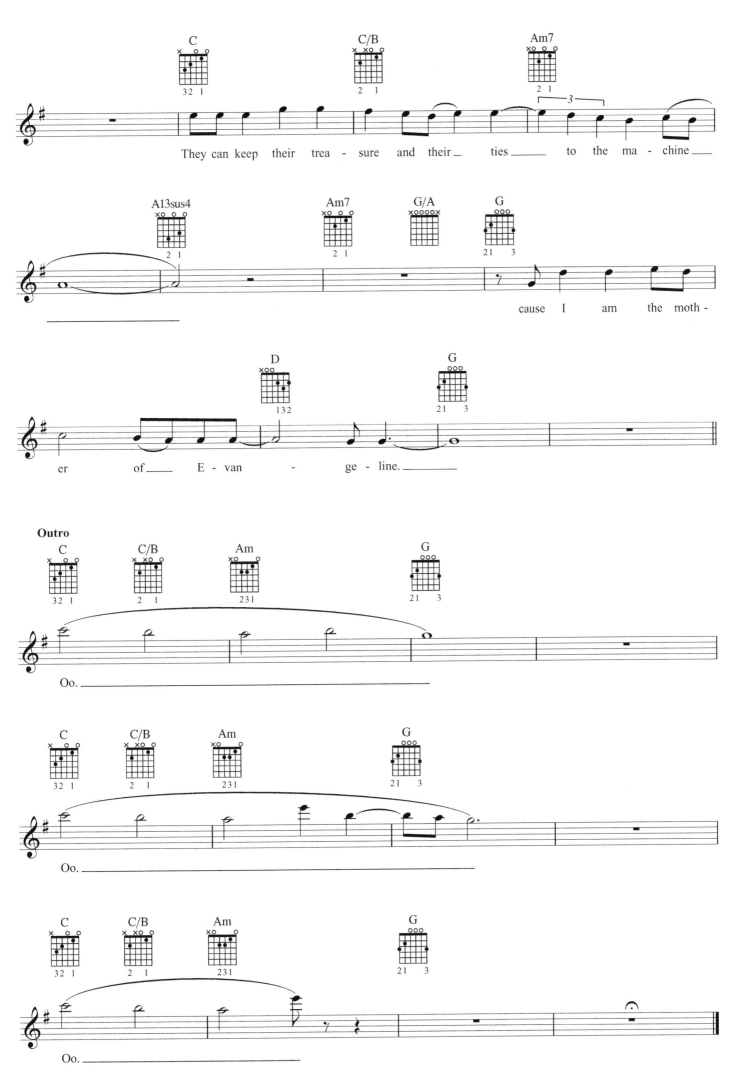

They can keep their trea - sure and their_ ties _____ to the ma - chine _____

cause I am the moth -

er of ___ E - van - ge - line. _____

Outro

Oo. _____

Oo. _____

Oo. _____

Whatever You Do

Words and Music by Brandi Carlile, Phil Hanseroth and Tim Hanseroth

mo - ment on - ly de - mons come to mind. _____ There are days _____

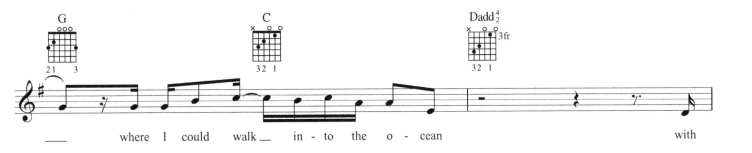

_____ where I could walk _____ in - to the o - cean with

D.S. al Coda

no one else _____ but you _____ to leave _____ be - hind. There's a

⊕ Coda

Chorus

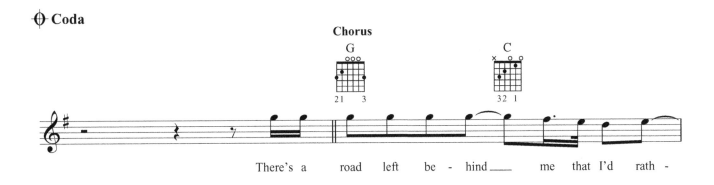

There's a road left be - hind _____ me that I'd rath -

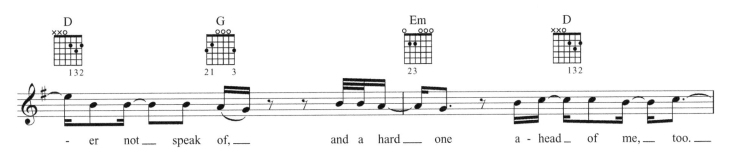

- er not _____ speak of, _____ and a hard _____ one a - head _____ of me, _____ too. _____

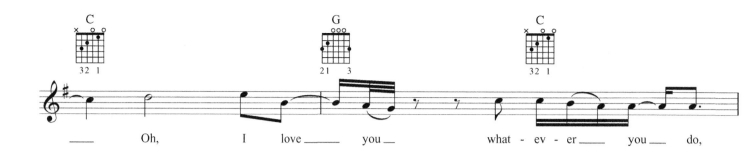

Oh, I love you whatever you do,

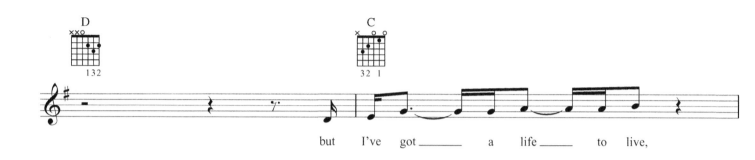

but I've got a life to live,

Outro
w/ Lead voc. ad lib

too.

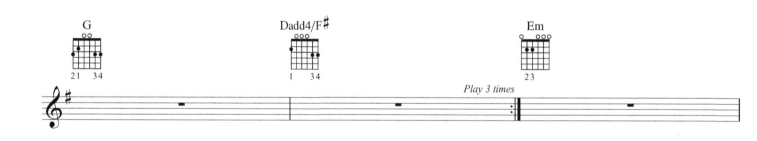

Play 3 times

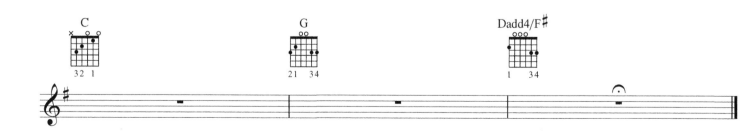

Fulton County Jane Doe

Words and Music by Brandi Carlile, Phil Hanseroth and Tim Hanseroth

Capo IV

Intro
Moderately slow ♩ = 86

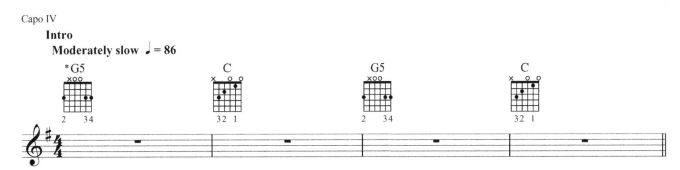

*All music sounds 2 steps higher than indicated due to capo.

Verse

1. Out in the mid - dle of no - where _____

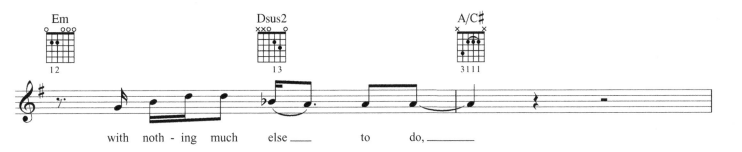

with noth - ing much else ___ to do, _____

oh, the night ___ brought us to - geth - er, _____

and I lent my heart _____ to you. _____

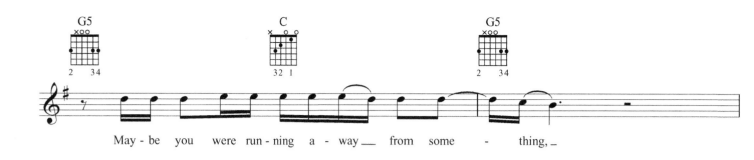

May - be you were run - ning a - way__ from some - thing,__

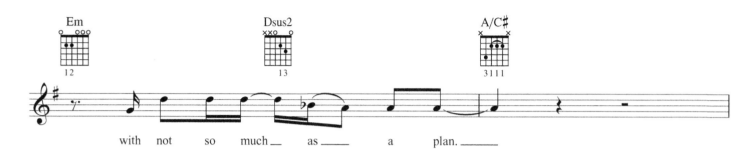

with not so much__ as__ a plan.__

Not a liv - ing__ soul__ to guide you;__

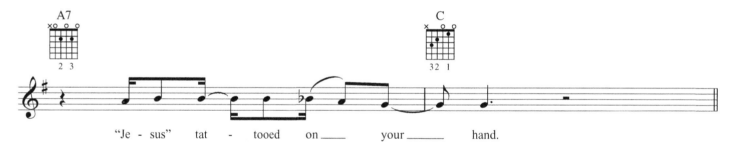

"Je - sus" tat - tooed on__ your__ hand.

Chorus

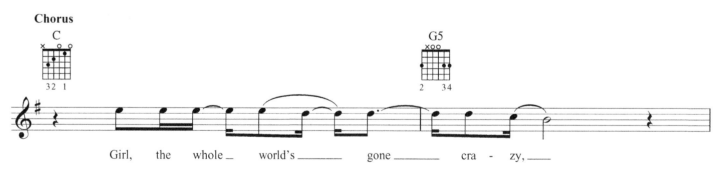

Girl, the whole__ world's__ gone__ cra - zy,__

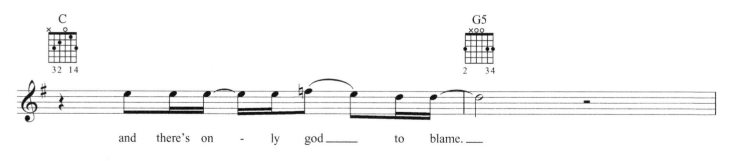

and there's on - ly god__ to blame.__

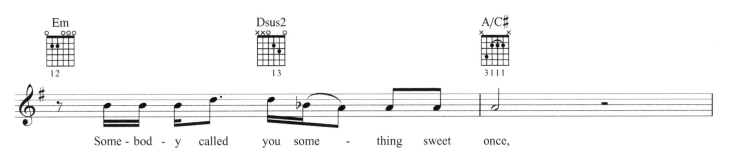

Some - bod - y called you some - thing sweet once,

Interlude

it was more than Ful - ton Coun - ty Jane.

Verse

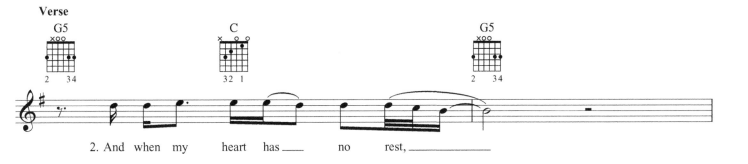

2. And when my heart has ___ no rest, _____

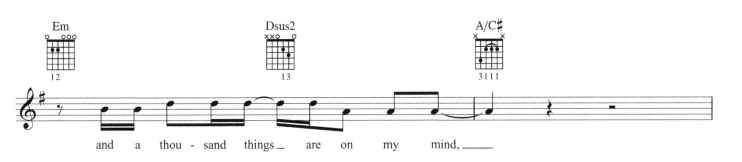

and a thou - sand things ___ are on my mind, _____

I'll al - ways save ___ some room ___ for you.

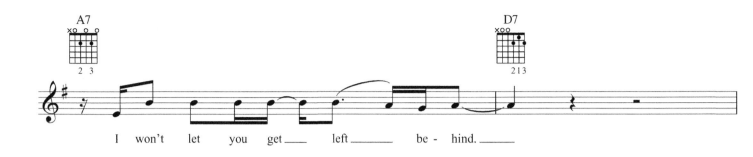

I won't let you get ___ left ___ be - hind. ___

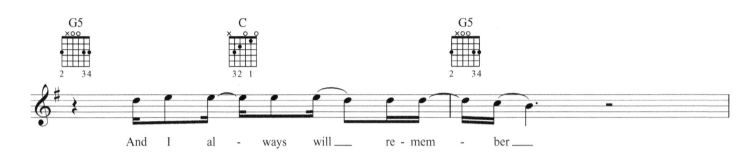

And I al - ways will ___ re - mem - ber ___

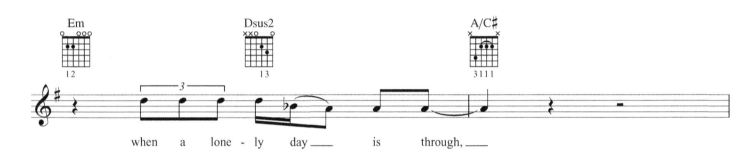

when a lone - ly day ___ is through, ___

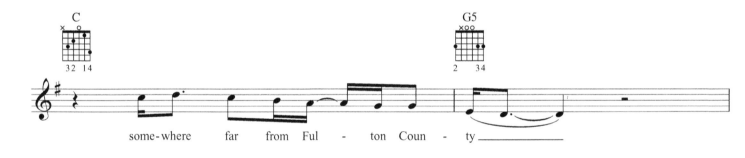

some-where far from Ful - ton Coun - ty ___

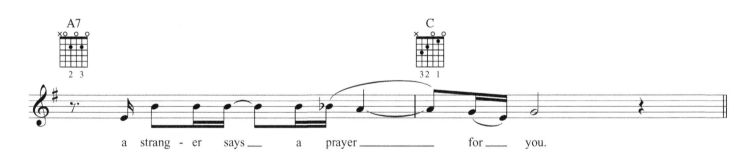

a strang - er says ___ a prayer ___ for ___ you.

Chorus

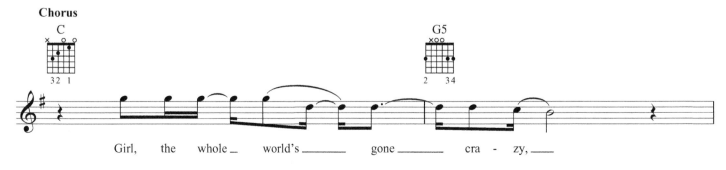

Girl, the whole ___ world's ___ gone ___ cra - zy, ___

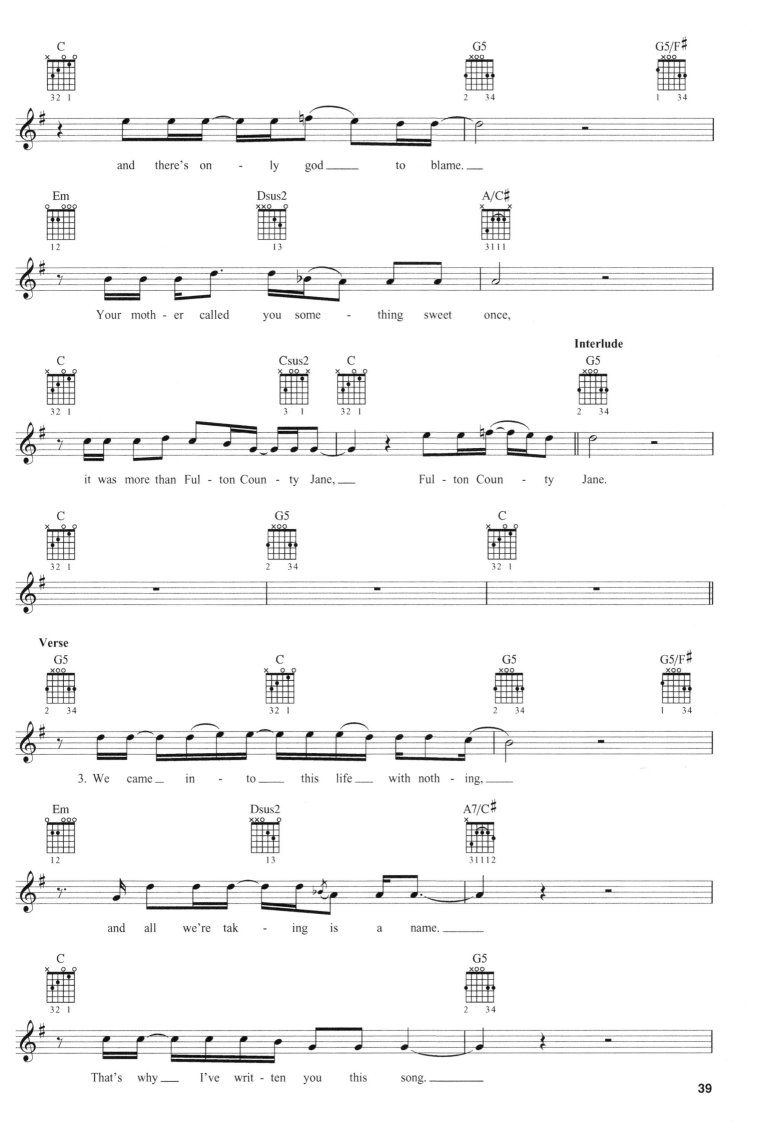

Sugartooth

Words and Music by Brandi Carlile, Phil Hanseroth and Tim Hanseroth

Verse

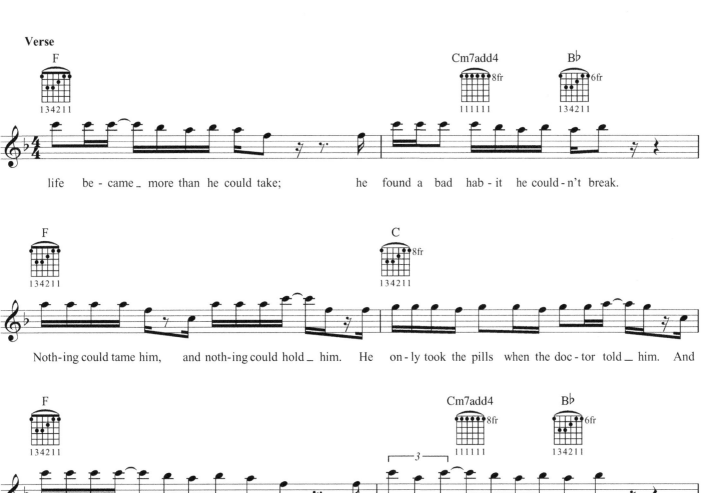

life be - came _ more than he could take; he found a bad hab - it he could - n't break.

Noth - ing could tame him, and noth - ing could hold _ him. He on - ly took the pills when the doc - tor told _ him. And

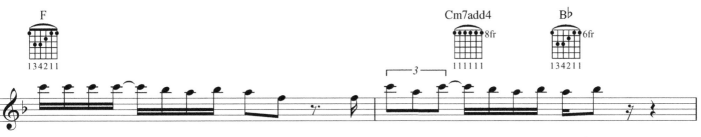

look - ing too hard _ for that some - thing sweet to make his life __ feel less in - com - plete.

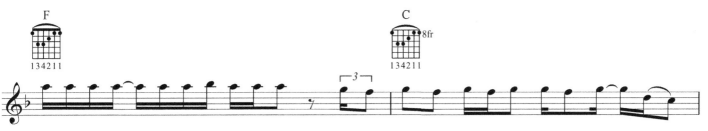

What in the hell __ are you go - ing to do when the world has made its mind up a - bout _ you? _

Chorus

He was a li - ar but not __ a fraud, _

liv - ing proof _ that there was _ no god, _____ just the dev - il stiff as a rod, _ a

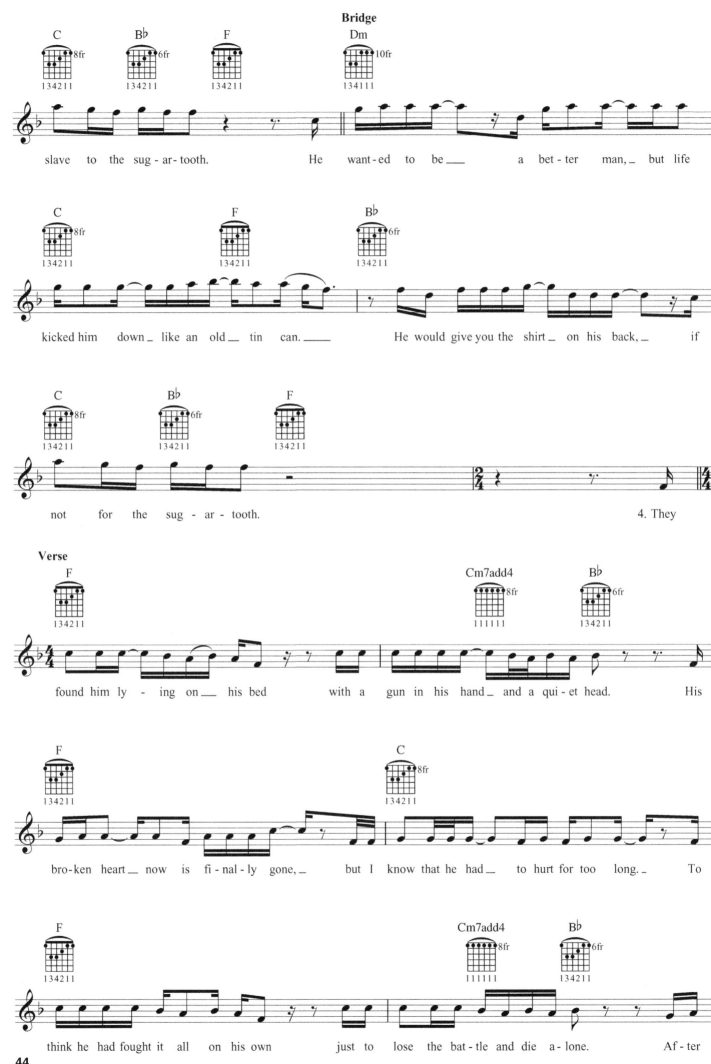

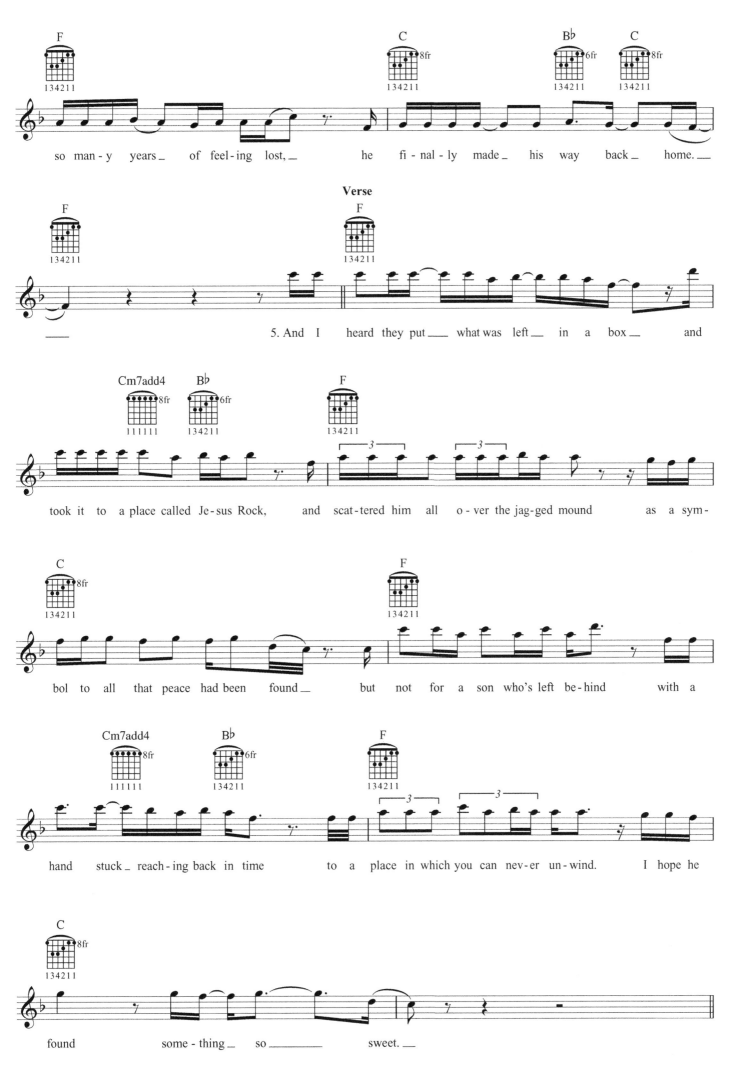

Chorus

He was a li - ar but not __ a fraud, __ liv - ing proof __ that there was __ no god, __

just the dev - il, stiff as a rod, __ a slave to the sug - ar - tooth. He

Bridge

want - ed to be __ a bet - ter man, __ but life kicked him down __ like an old __ tin __ can. ____

He would give you the shirt __ on his back, __ if not for the sug - ar - tooth.

Outro

Play 3 times

Oo, _____ oo, _____ oo, _____ a slave to the sug - ar - tooth.

rit.

Oo, _____ oo, _____ oo, _____ a slave to the sug - ar - tooth.

Most Of All

Words and Music by Brandi Carlile, Phil Hanseroth and Tim Hanseroth

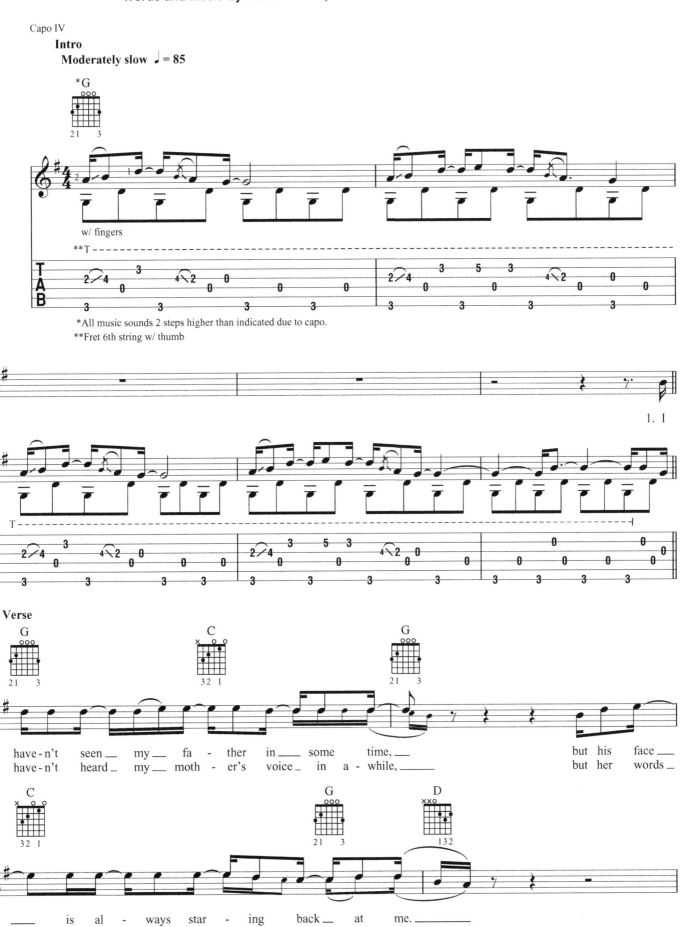

*All music sounds 2 steps higher than indicated due to capo.

**Fret 6th string w/ thumb

have - n't   seen ___ my ___ fa - ther   in ___ some   time, ___   but his   face ___
have - n't   heard ___ my ___ moth - er's   voice ___ in a - while, _____   but her   words ___

___   is al - ways   star - ing   back ___ at   me. _____
___   are al - ways   fall - ing   out   my ___   mouth. _____

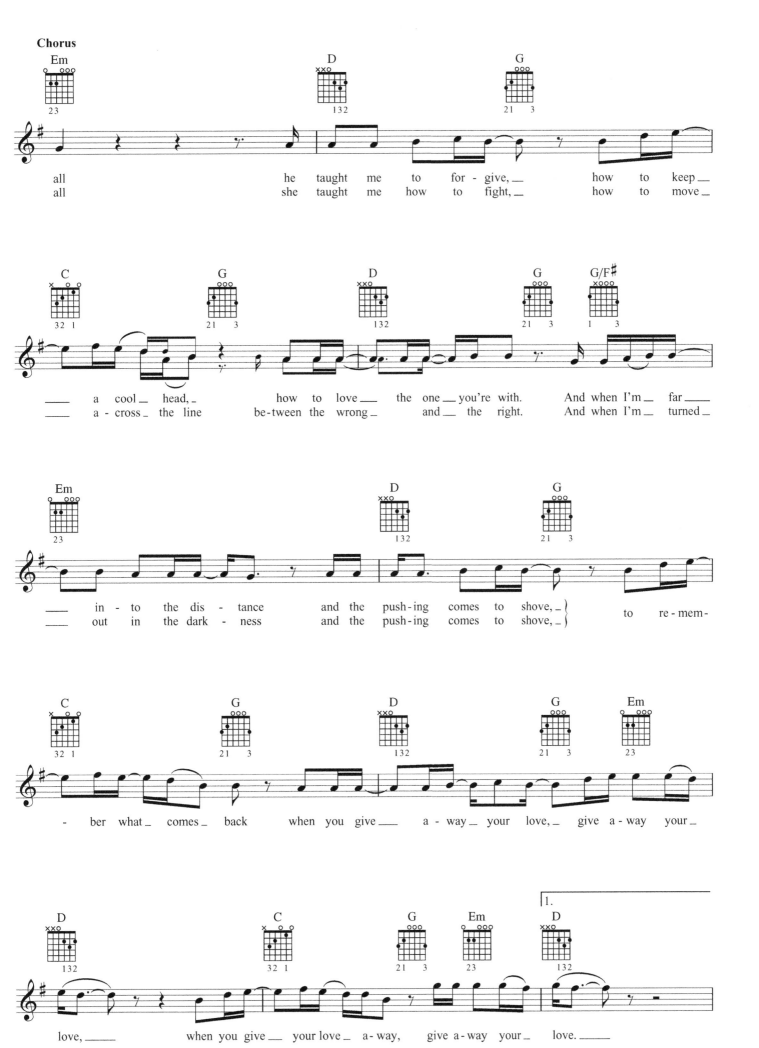

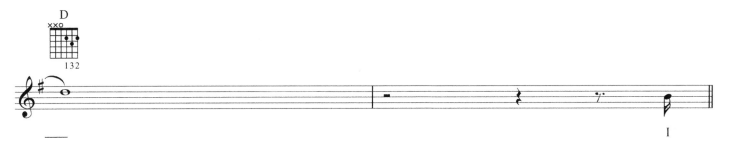

Outro

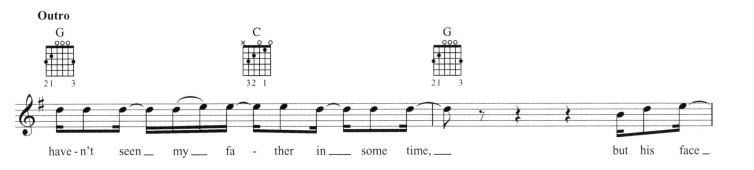

have-n't seen _ my _ fa - ther in _ some time, _ but his face _

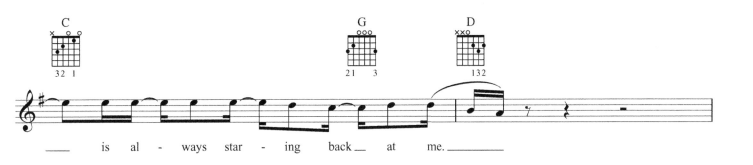

_ is al - ways star - ing back _ at me. _

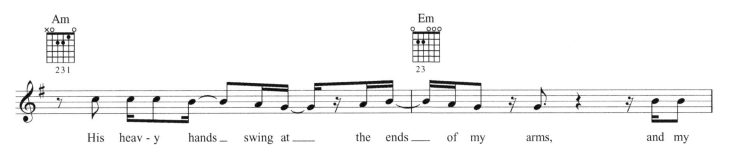

His heav-y hands _ swing at _ the ends _ of my arms, and my

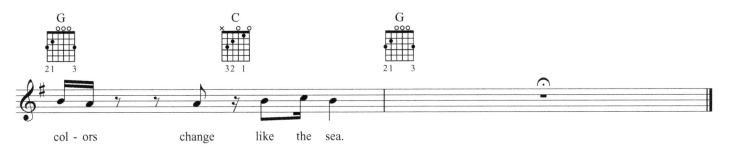

col - ors change like the sea.

Harder To Forgive

Words and Music by Brandi Carlile, Phil Hanseroth and Tim Hanseroth

hard - er ____ to for - give ____ than to ___ for - get.

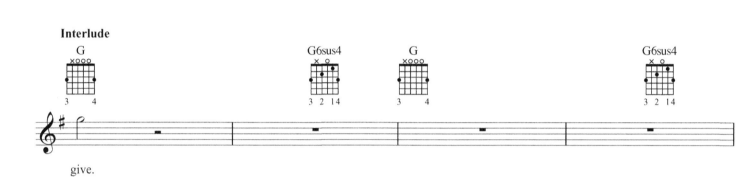

Some - times ___ it's hard - er ____ to for -

Interlude

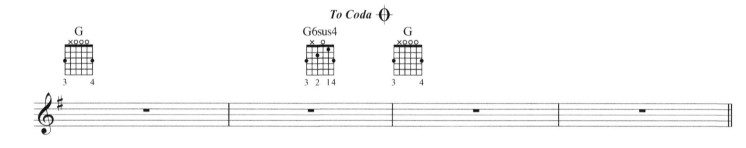

give.

To Coda ✦

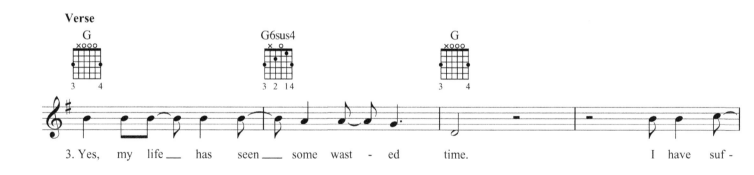

Verse

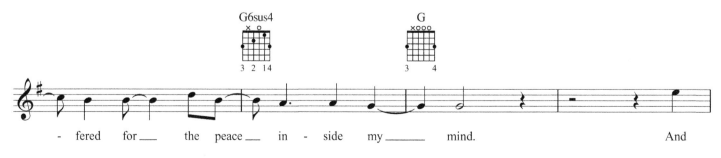

3. Yes, my life ___ has seen ___ some wast - ed time. I have suf -

- fered for ___ the peace ___ in - side my _____ mind. And

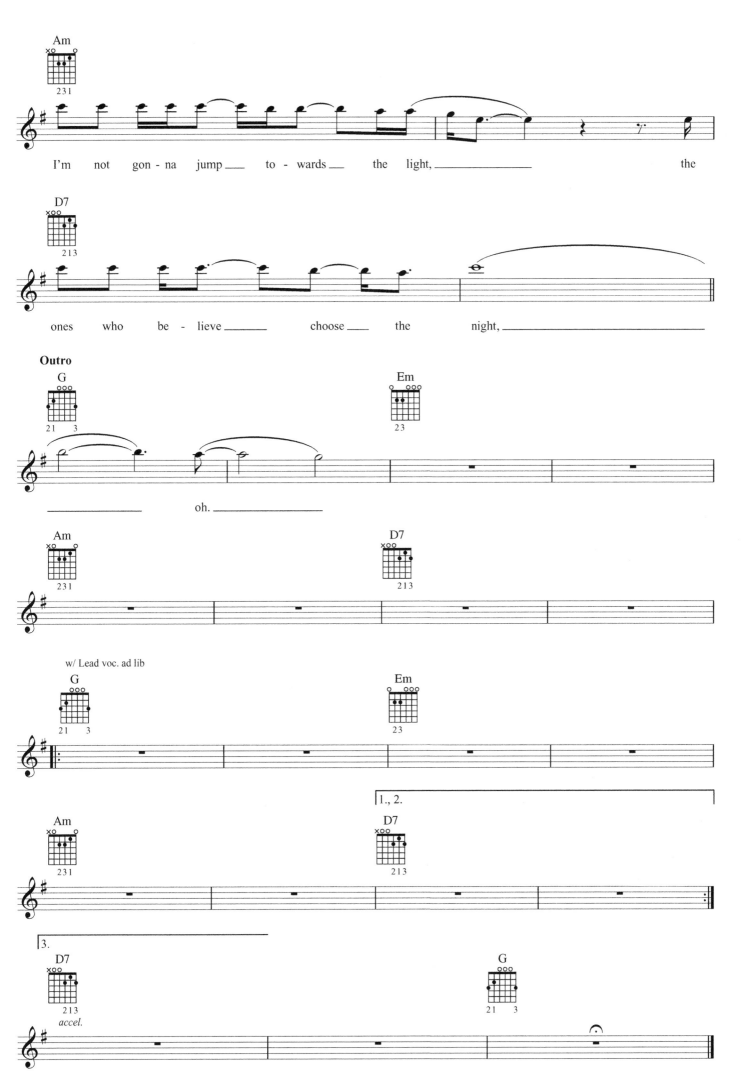

I'm not gon - na jump ___ to - wards ___ the light, _____ the

ones who be - lieve _____ choose ___ the night, _____

Outro

_____ oh. _____

w/ Lead voc. ad lib

1., 2.

3.

Party Of One

Words and Music by Brandi Carlile, Phil Hanseroth and Tim Hanseroth

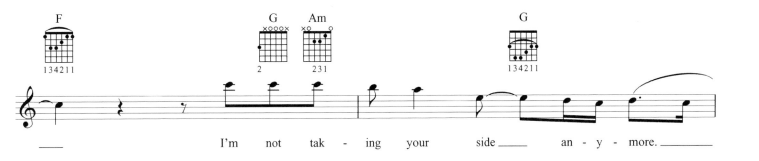

I'm not tak - ing your side ____ an - y - more. ____

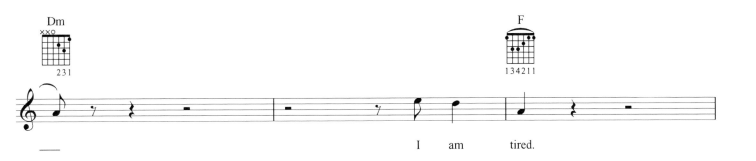

I am tired.

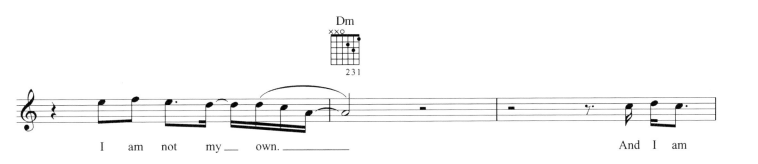

I am not my ___ own. _____ And I am

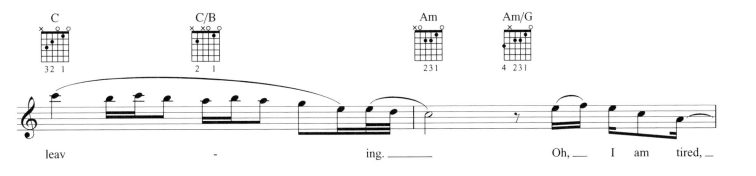

leav - ing. _____ Oh, ___ I am tired, __

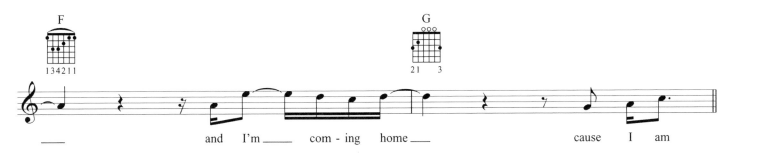

____ and I'm ___ com - ing home ___ cause I am